AF261454

The Adventures of Zoe the Zoo Bench

By: Nedia Lee

Hi, I am Zoe the Zoo Bench.
Come join me for a beautiful day at the zoo.
I wonder what we will see....
I am not sure, but I know we will see animals
that we can talk about with our family and friends.

Let us begin our journey at the zoo.

First, you have to pay to enter the zoo.
Make sure you have a little extra money
to buy food for the animals or refreshments for yourself
and your family.

Second, remember to follow the arrows.
They tell you what direction to go so you don't get lost.

Third, remember to read all the signs.
They give you information about the animals.
They also help you find the bathrooms, water fountains,
rest areas and places to buy food and refreshments.

Ready, here we go!

The first animals to welcome us are the monkeys.
Say, "Hello".

These monkeys are so excited
and want to show off their talents.
They like to groom each other,
cuddle, hold hands, bob their heads
and swing from tree to tree.

They love to eat bananas,
but also like to eat nuts, fruits, seeds and flowers.

Wow! I see Gorillas!

They like to interact with other gorillas.
They have hands and feet like humans.
They sleep at night in nests
and live to be around 35 years old.

Look over there! Giraffes!

Giraffes are the tallest mammals on Earth.
They have spots on their body. They can run very fast.
They only need to drink water once every few days.
They also only need 5 to 30 minutes of sleep each day.

Camels, Camels, Camels…..Camels everywhere….

There are two types of camels. There are one humped
and there are two humped camels.
They grunt and spit.
They can kick, buck, bite and even swat you with their tail.

Camels are known to be smarter than horses
and form close bonds with their humans.
They are intelligent and cute.

Lions! Tigers! Leopards! Oh my……

These are "BIG CATS".

Lions have long hair surrounding their necks, called manes. Lionesses do the hunting.

Tigers are the largest cat species on the planet. They are orange with black stripes.

Leopards have spotted fur. They hunt mostly at night.

Ready to see a Rhinoceros or two?
You can also call them Rhinos.

They are the second largest land mammals on Earth.
Rhinos have a large head, short legs and short tail.
They also can have one or two horns.
They can run fast. They are usually grey, black,
or brown. Some can even be white.

It's time to see the largest land animal on Earth.
The amazing elephant.

Elephants have long noses,
or trunks: large floppy ears; and wide, thick legs.

They are always hungry and sometimes
they use their tusks to help them eat.

They are very intelligent and have the largest brains.

Are you ready to see the world's largest bird?
It is the Ostrich.

An ostrich can not fly, but it can run very fast.
It has three stomachs and will eat roots, seeds and leaves.
They will sometimes eat locusts, lizards, snakes and rodents.

Ostriches are beautiful, but keep your distance.

I see pink everywhere! Pink! Pink! Pink!

Look at all the flamingos. They stick together in flocks.
They have long legs and long necks.
They spend most of their day feeding,
preening, resting and bathing.

Did you know that the flamingos' feathers, legs,
and face are colored by their diet?

Look! I see a blue flamingo!

Let's go visit the big bird house.

I see a woodpecker. Do you see a woodpecker?

I see a toucan. Do you see a toucan?

I see a bald eagle. Do you see a bald eagle?

I see a parrot. Do you see a parrot?

I see an owl. Do you see an owl?

I see a humming bird. Do you see a humming bird?

I see a falcon. Do you see a falcon?

I see a pelican. Do you see a pelican?

I see a duck. Do you see a duck?

I see a swan. Do you see a swan?

I see a crane. Do you see a crane?

There are so many types of birds.
Some are flying and some are swimming.
They are different colors and different sizes.

They brighten our world with their beauty
just like a peacock.

We had so much fun in the bird cage.
Let's see the animals that swim in the water.

Look at the turtles swimming
with all the many types of fish.
I even see alligators basking on the shore.

I think they are all friends.

I see penguins to my left and sea lions to my right.
These two animals can not be together.

I see a bigger area where the hippopotamus live.
You can also call them hippos.
They are the third-largest type of land mammal.
They stay in the water or mud to keep cool.
They eat grass on land and can run very fast.

Do you want to see other animals?

Look at the snakes, spiders, bugs and plants.
How many different types of animals and plants
do you see here?

There are so many animals to see at the zoo.
I only showed you just a few.
If there is a zoo near you.
You should drop in for a view.

Always remember that it doesn't matter
if the animals are tall or short,
big or small or even
what color they are...all animals matter to us
and have a purpose in this world.

I hope you liked our adventure at the zoo.
If you are looking for another adventure,
look for my friend, Selena.
She is Selena the Seashore Bench.
You will see amazing things with her at the beach.

www.ingramcontent.com/pod-product-compliance
Lightning Source LLC
Chambersburg PA
CBHW042204030726
47602CB00007B/115